What's in this book

This book belongs to

_____

花与果 Flowers and fruit

学习内容 Contents

沟通 Communication

说说花和果实
Talk about flowers and fruit

生词 New words

★	甜	sweet
★	草莓	strawberry
★	梨	pear
★	得	(used between a verb and its complement to indicate the degree)
★	桃子	peach
★	香蕉	banana
★	有意思	interesting
★	看见	to see
★	盘	(measure word for dishes)
	跟	and
	粉红色	pink
	棕色	brown

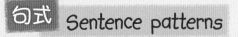

句式 Sentence patterns

梨比草莓大得多。

A pear is much bigger than a strawberry.

花开得美。

Flowers are so beautiful.

跨学科学习 Project

种植草莓，并用图表记录它的生长

Grow some strawberries and record their growth

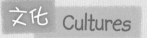

文化 Cultures

和水果相关的中文和英文成语

Chinese and English idioms related to fruit

Get ready

1 What is your favourite fruit?

2 Have you ever seen the flowers of that fruit?

3 Do you know the flowers and fruit in the picture?

tián

甜

你知道这是什么水果的花吗？这种
水果红红的，很甜。

lí
梨

de
得

gēn
跟

cǎo méi
草莓

这是草莓。草莓的花跟梨的花有点儿
像，但是梨比草莓大得多。

táo zi
桃子

zōng sè
棕色

fěn hóng sè
粉红色

桃子长在棕色的树枝上，它的花是
粉红色或者白色的。

有意思
yǒu yì si

香蕉
xiāng jiāo

香蕉的花很有意思，它又大又红，
跟香蕉不像。

大自然真奇妙！花开得美，不同的花结出不同的果实。

当你看见这盘水果时，想过它们
生长的故事吗？

Let's think

1 Recall the story. Match the fruits to their flowers.

2 Make an interesting breakfast and describe it. Paste your photo below.

这只狮子真有意思！它的眼睛是葡萄，鼻子是桃子，脸上还有草莓。我喜欢这只水果狮子！你做的是什么呢？

Paste your photo here.

这是我做的……

New words

1 Learn the new words.

看见

桃子

盘

草莓

粉红色

甜

香蕉

有意思

棕色

梨

得

跟

2 Listen to your teacher and point to the correct words above.

听听说说 Listen and say

1 水果蛋糕里没有哪个水果?

   a 草莓

   b 香蕉

   c 梨

2 爸爸买了什么颜色的花?

   a 粉红色

   b 粉红色或红色

   c 粉红色和红色

3 他们跟妈妈说了有水果蛋糕和花吗?

   a 说了

   b 没说

   c 正在说

4 他们为什么做蛋糕? 为什么买花?

   a 因为今天是妈妈的生日。

   b 因为今天休息。

   c 因为今天天气好。

04 🎧 **2** Look at the pictures. Listen to the story

①

这些是我新买的水果,很甜。

今天的草莓比前天的大得多。

③

你怎么不吃?

我想等到晚上吃。

为什么?

 这里还有梨和葡萄。

 这些都是我喜欢的水果。

 我想等爸爸和弟弟回来再吃，大家一起吃比一个人吃高兴得多。

3 Write the letters and say.

a 得　b 跟　c 有意思　d 看见

1

爸爸＿＿＿爷爷的样子有点儿像，但爸爸比爷爷高＿＿＿多。

2

我＿＿＿长颈鹿和斑马在喝水。

我喜欢带小狗去海边玩，我觉得很＿＿＿。

3

13

Task

Paste the photos of the flowers of the apple and grapes below. Talk about the fruit with your friend.

这是苹果，它生长在……它的花……

草莓生长在地上。先开出白色的花，花开得很漂亮，然后长出红色的草莓。草莓不大，但是很甜。

Paste your photo here.

Paste your photo here.

这是葡萄跟葡萄的花……

Game

Follow the two food paths and find out what they lead to. Colour the food as you go along. Talk about the pictures and say the names of the food with your friend.

开始

你有健康的牙齿。你笑得真漂亮！

你要去看牙医！

我用／不用去看牙医，因为我画了……然后画了……我喜欢吃……跟……

Chant

 05 Listen and say.

香蕉长，桃子圆，
草莓小，梨子大。

香蕉的花是红色的，
桃子的花是粉红色的，
草莓的花是白色的，
梨的花也是白色的。

花开得多，开得好，
水果长得大，长得好。

生活用语 Daily expressions

有意思。
It's interesting.

没意思。
It's boring.

写一写 Write

1 Trace and write the characters.

ˊ ˊ 彳 彳 彳 彳 彳 得 得 得

得	得		

一 ナ 才 冇 有 有

亠 亠 亠 立 产 音 音 音 意 意 意

丶 丨 囗 囗 田 田 思 思 思

有	意	思	有	意	思

2 Write and say.

这是我最喜欢吃的糖果，它是粉红色的，比草莓甜___多。

真_____!
我还想再玩儿一次。

3 Fill in the blanks with the correct words. Colour the horses using the same colours.

站

看见

得

有意思

昨天，爸爸妈妈带我去看跑马。我 _____ 很多马，棕色跟黑色的都有，它们都很漂亮。

跑马开始后，马都跑 ___ 很快。我 _____ 骑马的人 ___ 着， _____ 很高。跑马真 _____ ！

拼音输入法 Pinyin input

Fill in the blanks. Number the sentences to make a meaningful paragraph. Type the paragraph and read it to your friend.

◯ 我会中文，我已经学了 ___ 年。

◯ 但是中文很有 ___ 思，我喜欢学。

◯ 开始学 ___ 文时，我觉得它很难。

◯ 我也能打更多汉字。我真喜欢中文！

◯ 现在，我能写很多汉字，还写 ___ 很好。

Cultures

1 Learn about two Chinese idioms that are related to fruit.

我们应该学会孔融让梨。

我长大了，也想做一个好老师，可以桃李满门。

In ancient China, Kong Rong, a four-year-old boy, gave the larger pears to his brothers and saved the smaller one for himself. His act exemplified the value of courtesy and humility that a child should have and hence the idiom 孔融让梨 (kǒng róng ràng lí).

桃李满门 (táo lǐ mǎn mén) refers to a respected teacher having lots of good students all around the world.

2 Some English idioms are also about fruit. Write the correct letters.

a 苹果 b 有用 c 没用 d 生气 e 香蕉

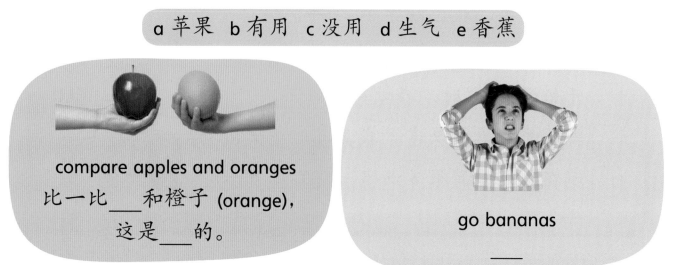

compare apples and oranges
比一比＿＿和橙子 (orange)，
这是＿＿的。

go bananas

＿＿

1 Do you know how to grow strawberries? Research and number the pictures.

sunlight

air

草莓的生长，要有阳光 (sunlight)、空气 (air) 和水。

2 It's your turn now. Grow some strawberries and record their growth. Then report to your classmates.

a 晴天　b 刮风　c 下雨　d 下雪　e 多云

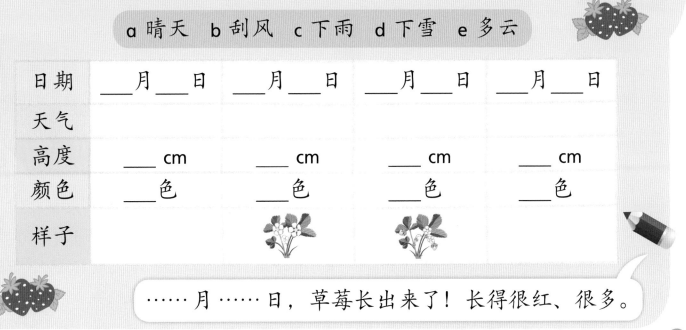

日期	___月___日	___月___日	___月___日	___月___日
天气				
高度	___ cm	___ cm	___ cm	___ cm
颜色	__色	__色	__色	__色
样子				

……月……日，草莓长出来了！长得很红、很多。

1 Know more about yourself. Complete the questionnaire. Read the question
and tick the boxes. Then calculate your score.

		a never	b sometimes	c of
1	你吃饭前会洗手吗？	☐	☐	☐
2	你吃水果吃得多吗？	☐	☐	☐
3	你吃蔬菜吃得多吗？	☐	☐	☐
4	你吃甜的食物吃得多吗？	☐	☐	☐
5	你晚上会睡十个小时吗？	☐	☐	☐
6	你看电视看得多吗？	☐	☐	☐
7	你玩电脑玩得多吗？	☐	☐	☐
8	你做运动做得多吗？	☐	☐	☐
9	你骑自行车骑得多吗？	☐	☐	☐
10	你会走路上学吗？	☐	☐	☐

计分表

1	a 1	b 2	c 3	d 4	6	a 4	b 3	c 2	d 1
2	a 1	b 2	c 3	d 4	7	a 4	b 3	c 2	d 1
3	a 1	b 2	c 3	d 4	8	a 1	b 2	c 3	d 4
4	a 4	b 3	c 2	d 1	9	a 1	b 2	c 3	d 4
5	a 1	b 2	c 3	d 4	10	a 1	b 2	c 3	d 4

分析

32–40 你真健康！

23–31 你有一点儿不健康。

14–22 你不太健康。

我有……分。我很喜欢吃水果，草莓、香蕉、桃子跟梨，我都喜欢吃。我有时候会玩飞盘，但是我很少运动。所以我有一点儿不健康。你呢？

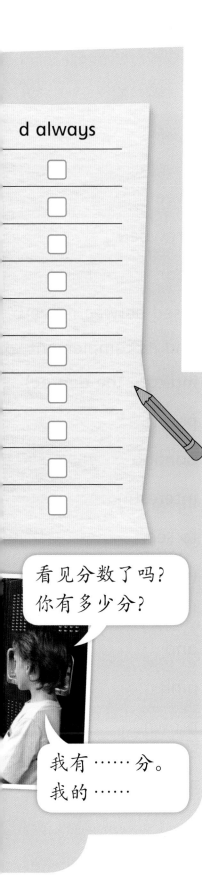

d always

□
□
□
□
□
□
□
□
□
□

看见分数了吗？
你有多少分？

我有……分。
我的……

2 Work with your friend. Colour the stars and the chillies.

Words and sentences	说	读	写
甜	☆	☆	🌶
草莓	☆	☆	🌶
梨	☆	☆	🌶
得	☆	☆	☆
桃子	☆	☆	🌶
香蕉	☆	☆	🌶
有意思	☆	☆	☆
看见	☆	☆	🌶
盘	☆	☆	🌶
跟	☆	🌶	🌶
粉红色	☆	🌶	🌶
棕色	☆	🌶	🌶
梨比草莓大得多。	☆	🌶	🌶
花开得美。	☆	🌶	🌶

Talk about flowers and fruit	☆

3 What does your teacher say?

分享 Sharing

Words I remember

甜	tián	sweet
草莓	cǎo méi	strawberry
梨	lí	pear
得	de	(used between a verb and its complement to indicate the degree)
桃子	táo zi	peach
香蕉	xiāng jiāo	banana
有意思	yǒu yì si	interesting
看见	kàn jiàn	to see
盘	pán	(measure word for dishes)
跟	gēn	and
粉红色	fěn hóng sè	pink
棕色	zōng sè	brown

Other words

果实	guǒ shí	fruit
长	zhǎng	to grow
树枝	shù zhī	branch
奇妙	qí miào	amazing
开	kāi	to open out
结	jié	to form
出	chū	to put forth
当	dāng	when
过	guò	(auxiliary word of tense)
生长	shēng zhǎng	to grow
故事	gù shi	story
孔融让梨	kǒng róng ràng lí	(to show the value of courtesy and humility)
桃李满门	táo lǐ mǎn mén	(a respected teacher with lots of good students)
橙子	chéng zi	orange
阳光	yáng guāng	sunlight
空气	kōng qì	air

OXFORD
UNIVERSITY PRESS

Oxford University Press is a department of the University of Oxford.
It furthers the University's objective of excellence in research, scholarship,
and education by publishing worldwide. Oxford is a registered trade mark of
Oxford University Press in the UK and in certain other countries

Published in Hong Kong by
Oxford University Press (China) Limited
39th Floor, One Kowloon, 1 Wang Yuen Street, Kowloon Bay,
Hong Kong

Illustrated by Anne Lee, Emily Chan and Wildman

Photographs for reproduction permitted by Dreamstime.com

China National Publications Import & Export (Group) Corporation is an authorized distributor of
Oxford Elementary Chinese.

Please contact content@cnpiec.com.cn or 86-10-65856782

ISBN: 978-0-19-082314-6

10 9 8 7 6 5 4 3 2